2013 GREATEST Pop & Movie Hits

W9-ATZ-790

THE BIGGEST MOVIES ★ THE GREATEST ARTISTS

DELUXE ANNUAL EDITION

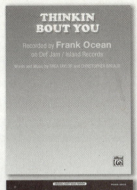

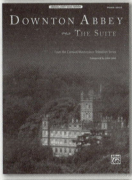

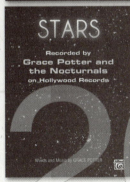

Alfred

Produced by
Alfred Music Publishing Co., Inc.
P.O. Box 10003
Van Nuys, CA 91410-0003

alfred.com

Printed in USA.

ISBN-10: 0-7390-9623-0
ISBN-13: 978-0-7390-9623-9

WITHDRAWN

 Alfred Cares. Contents printed on 100% recycled paper.

CONTENTS

ANYTHING COULD HAPPEN

Words and Music by
ELLIE GOULDING and JAMES ELIOT

Moderate pop rock ♩ = 102

Verse 2:

2. Af - ter the war we said we'd fight to - geth - er.

I guess we thought that's just what hu - mans do,___

___ let - ting dark-ness grow, as if we need it's pal -

whoa.___

But I don't think I need

CATCH MY BREATH

Words and Music by
JASON HALBERT, KELLY CLARKSON
and ERIC OLSON

Moderately fast pop rock ♩ = 126

BLOWN AWAY

Words and Music by
JOSH KEAR
and CHRIS TOMPKINS

Moderately bright ♩ = 140

Verse 1:

1. Dry light-ning cracks a-cross the skies.

Those storm clouds gath-er in her eyes.

Blown Away - 8 - 1

22 *Chorus:*

blown a - way._____

Verse 2:

2. She heard those si - rens scream - ing out._____

Her dad - dy laid there passed out on the couch._____

She__locked her - self in the cel - lar, lis-tened to the scream-ing of__ the wind.

24

Some peo-ple call it tak - ing___ shel -ter; she called it sweet___ re - venge.___

Chorus:

Shat -ter ev - ery win - dow 'til it's all blown a -way.___ Ev - ery

brick, ev - ery board, ev - ery slam -ming door, blown a - way___ 'til there's

noth-ing left stand - ing, noth-ing left of yes - ter -day.___ Ev - ery

Chorus:

Shat-ter ev-ery win-dow 'til it's all blown a-way._____ Ev-ery

brick, ev-ery board, ev-ery slam-ming door, blown a-way_____ 'til there's

noth-ing left stand-ing, noth-ing left of yes-ter-day._____ Ev-ery

tear-soaked whis-key mem-o-ry blown a-way,_____ blown a-way.__

DOWNTON ABBEY - THE SUITE

Composed by
JOHN LUNN

Allegro con spirito ♩ = 165

Downton Abbey - The Suite - 14 - 1

Tempo I (♩. = 112)

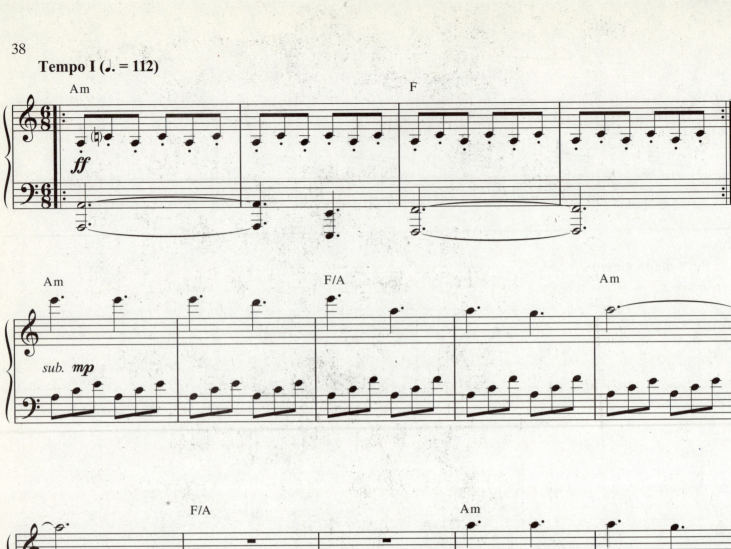

40

EVERYBODY TALKS

Words and Music by
TYLER GLENN and TIM PAGNOTTA

Moderately fast rock ♩ = 152

Verse 1:

44

Verse 2:

2. Hey, hon-ey, you could be my drug.__ You could be my new__ pre-scrip-tion.__

Too much could be an o-ver-dose.____ All this trash talk make__ me itch-in'._____ Oh, my, my, s***,

ev-'ry-bod-y talks, ev-'ry-bod-y talks, ev-'ry-bod-y talks *too much*. It start-ed with a

FALLING SLOWLY

Words and Music by
GLEN HANSARD and
MARKÉTA IRGLOVÁ

Slowly ♩ = 69

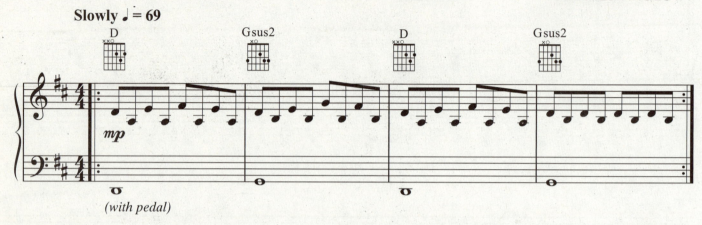

(with pedal)

Verse 1:

1. I don't know you, but I want you all the more for that.

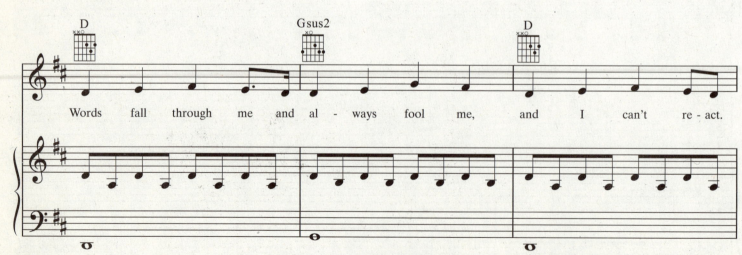

Words fall through me and al - ways fool me, and I can't re - act.

Falling Slowly - 5 - 1

self. It's time that you won, won._____ So

Chorus:

Take this sink - in' boat and point it home, we've still got time._____

Raise your hope - ful voice, you have a choice, you've made it now._____

Bridge:

GIRL ON FIRE

Words and Music by
BILLY SQUIER, JEFFREY BHAKSER,
ALICIA KEYS and SALAAM REMI

Moderately, with a heavy beat ♩ = 92

Verse 1: (Sing first time only)

1. She's just a girl, and she's on fi - re.

Verse 2: (Sing second time only)

2. Looks like a girl, but she's a flame.

Hot - ter than a fan - ta - sy, lone - ly like a high - way.

So bright, she can burn your eyes, bet - ter look the oth - er way.

Girl on Fire - 7 - 1

Bridge:

Ev-'ry-bod-y stands as she goes by, 'cause they can see the flame that's in her eyes.
oh, oh,

Watch her as she's light-in' up the night.
oh,
No-bod-y knows that she's a lone-
oh.

ly girl, and it's a lone-ly world. But she gon' let it
Oh,

Chorus:

GOOD MORNING BEAUTIFUL

Words and Music by
JIM BRICKMAN and LUKE McMASTER

Bridge:

La la la la la la la la.

Verse 3:

3. Some-times this world_ is such a cra - zy place,_ but all I need_ is just to see_ your face._

_ Wheth-er sun - shine or wheth-er the rain,_ I can weath-er an - y weath-er with

Chorus:

Bridge:

70

GOOD TIME

Words and Music by
MATTHEW THIESSEN,
BRIAN LEE and ADAM YOUNG

Moderate dance tempo ♩ = 120

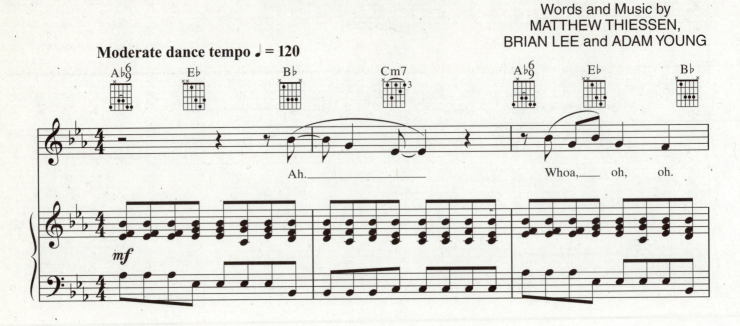

Ah._____ Whoa,___ oh, oh.

It's al - ways a good time.___ Whoa,___ oh, oh. It's al - ways a good time.____

Verse 1:

(Synth)

1. Woke up on the

Good Time - 6 - 1

down to get down to-night,___ 'cuz it's al-ways a good time.___ }
down to get down to-night,___ 'cuz it's al-ways a good time.___ }

Good morn-ing and good - night.___ I wake up at twi-

light.___ It's gon-na be al - right.___

Chorus:

We don't e-ven have to try, it's al-ways a good time.___ Whoa,___ oh, oh.

HARD TO LOVE

Words and Music by
BILLY MONTANA,
JOHN OZIER and BEN GLOVER

Hard to Love - 7 - 1

Verse:

1. I am in-sen-si-tive, I have a ten-den-cy to
2. I am a short fuse, I am a wreck-ing ball,

pay more at-ten-tion to the things that I need.___
crash - ing in-to your heart like I do.___

Some-times I drink too___ much, some-times I test your___ trust.
You're like a Sun-day morn-ing, full of grace, and full of Je - sus.

Some-times I don't know why you stay___ with me.___ } I'm hard to
I wish that I could be - more___ like you.___

Chorus:

love, hard to love, oh, I don't make it eas - y. I could-n't do it if I

stood where you stood.__ I'm hard to love,_ hard to love,_____ you say that you need__ me._____

1.

Well, I don't de-serve it, but I love that you love__ me good._____

Bridge:

83

Hard to Love - 7 - 6

You love me good.____

HOME

Words and Music by
DREW PEARSON and GREG HOLDEN

Moderately ♩ = 120

Verse 1:

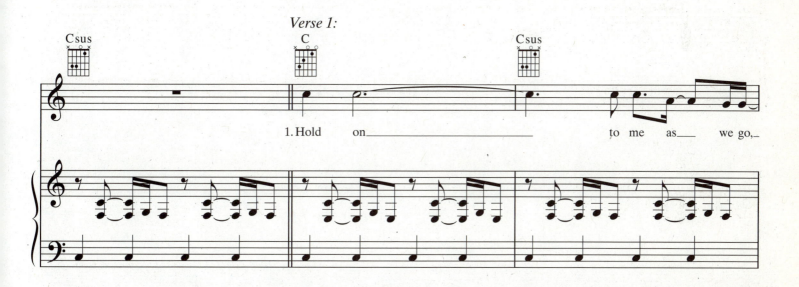

1. Hold on_____ to me as__ we go,__

__ as we roll down__

Home - 5 - 1

down. You_ get lost, you_ can al-ways_ be found. Just

know you're not a-lone,___ 'cause I'm gon-na

make this place your___ home.

Bridge:

1. Ooh,_____ ooh.___
2.3.4.5. Ah,_____ oh,___ ah,___ oh.___

LIGHTS

Words and Music by
ELLIE GOULDING, RICHARD STANNARD
and ASHLEY HOWES

lights, lights, lights, lights,

lights, lights.) Home, home.

You show the

Home, home, home.

Home,—

home.

LOCKED OUT OF HEAVEN

Words and Music by
PHILIP LAWRENCE,
BRUNO MARS and ARI LEVINE

Moderately bright ♩ = 144

Oh, yeah,___ yeah, oh yeah,___ yeah, yeah,___ yeah. *Oo.* Oh, yeah,___ yeah, oh yeah,___ yeah, yeah,___ yeah. *Oo.*

Locked Out of Heaven - 7 - 1

Verse 1: (Sing first time only)

Verse 2: (Sing second time only)

THE MISSION

(from *Argo*)

By
ALEXANDRE DESPLAT

The Mission - 3 - 1

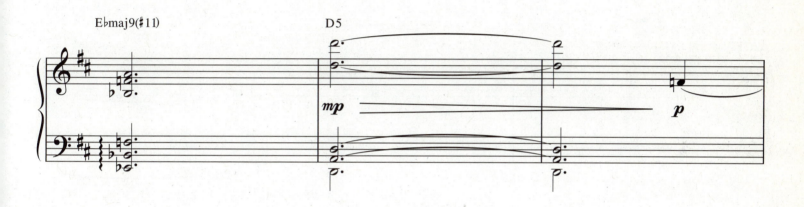

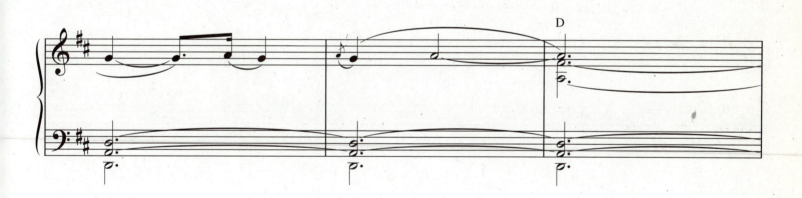

MISTY MOUNTAINS

(from *The Hobbit: An Unexpected Journey*)

Lyrics by
J.R.R. TOLKIEN

Music by
DAVID DONALDSON, DAVID LONG,
STEVE ROCHE and JANET RODDICK

Moderate chant, sung freely (♩ = 104)

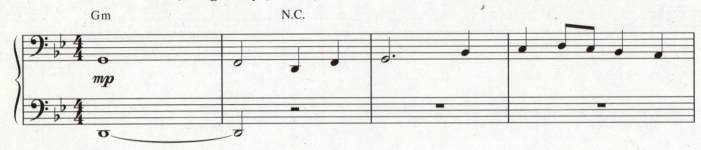

Austerely

Far o-

ver the Mist - y_____ Moun - tains cold

*Vocal sung one octave lower.

A THOUSAND YEARS

Words and Music by
DAVID HODGES
and CHRISTINA PERRI

Time has brought your heart to me. I have loved you for a thou - sand years. I'll love you for a

thou - sand more.

One step

Chorus:

SILVER LINING
(Crazy 'Bout You)

Words and Music by
DIANE WARREN

Rubato

Call me____ cra - zy.____

Moderate pop rock ♩ = 100

Verse 1:

1. In a world where no one, no one un - der - stands,____ it's good to fin - 'lly find some-

one, some-one who can. You know____ me____ bet - ter than I know my - self.

*Original recording in F♯ major.

Verse 1 cont. (Sing 1st time only):

Don't care what they say, don't care what this world thinks. We got each oth - er, that's all

Verse 2 (Sing 2nd time only):

2. When I lose my mind, when I'm a to - tal mess, I smile 'cuz you still think I'm

(Opt. bass 2nd time)

we need. And you show me I don't need noth - ing else.

the best. And I love you e - ven when you're a wreck.

Call me cra - zy, call me a fool.

Call me cra - zy, call me a fool.

STARS

Words and Music by
GRACE POTTER

Moderately slow ♩ = 72

(with pedal)

Verse:

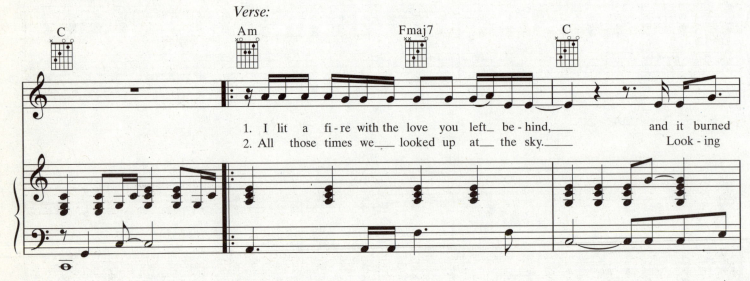

1. I lit a fi - re with the love you left_ be - hind,_____ and it burned
2. All those times we_____ looked up at_ the sky._____ Look - ing

wild_____ and crept_ up the moun - tain_ side._____
out_ so far,_ it_ felt like we_ could_ fly._____

know you at all,___ I know you've gone too__ far.___ So I,___ I can't look at the

stars.___

Guitar solo:

Chorus:

Stars,_____ stars,_____ they make_ me won-der where_ you are._____ Stars,_____ up_ on_ heav-en's boul-e-vard.___ And if I___ know you at all,_____ I know you've gone_ too_ far._____ So,__ I can't look at the stars.

Slower, rubato

rall.

THINKIN BOUT YOU

Words and Music by
SHEA TAYLOR
and CHRISTOPHER BREAUX

Slowly ♩ = 63

Verse 1: (Sing first time only)

na - do flew a - round my room be-fore you came. Ex-cuse the mess it made, it us - 'lly does-n't rain in

Verse 2: (Sing second time only)

like you, I just thought you were cool e-nough to kick it. Got a beach house I could sell you in I - da-ho. Since you think I don't

South-ern Cal-i - for - ian, much like A-ri-zo - na. My eyes don't shed tears but boy, they bawl when I'm

love you, I just thought you were cute, that's why I kissed you. Got-ta fight-er jet, I don't get to fly it, though. I'm ly-in' down

A VERY RESPECTABLE HOBBIT

(from *The Hobbit: An Unexpected Journey*)

Music by
HOWARD SHORE

A Very Respectable Hobbit - 2 - 1

WHEN I WAS YOUR MAN

Words and Music by
PHILIP LAWRENCE, ANDREW WYATT,
BRUNO MARS and ARI LEVINE

Moderately slow, with a bounce ♩ = 76

Verse 1: (Sing first time only)

1. Same bed but it feels just a lit-tle bit big-ger now,

Verse 2: (Sing second time only)

2. My pride, my e-go, my needs and my self-ish ways

our song on the ra-di-o, but it don't sound the same.

'caused a good strong wom-an like you to walk out my life. Now I'll

Chorus:

TWO BLACK CADILLACS

Words and Music by
CARRIE UNDERWOOD, JOSH KEAR
and HILLARY LINDSEY

Moderately ♩ = 116

Verse 1 (Sing 1st time only):

1. Two black Ca-dil-lacs driv-in' in a slow pa-rade;___

Verse 2 (Sing 2nd time only):

2. Two months a-go,___ his wife called the num-ber on his phone.___

head-lights shin-in' bright in the mid-dle of the day.___

Turns out he'd___ been lying to both of them for oh, so___ long.___

Two Black Cadillacs - 7 - 1

rose down,__ threw a hand - ful of dirt in - to the deep ground.__ He's__

__ not the on - ly__ one who had a se - cret to hide.__ Bye bye,__

__ bye bye,__ bye__ bye,_____

_____ yeah, yeah,__ yeah, yeah,_____ yeah._____

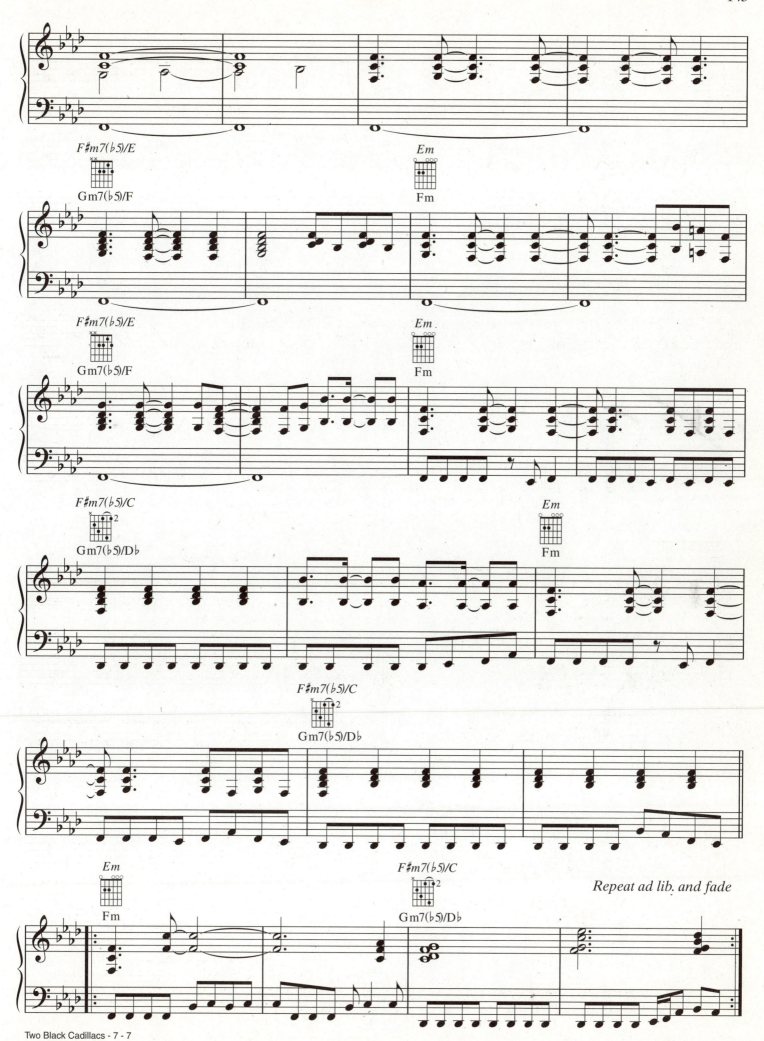